Beautiful Baubles

Illustrated by

L. Jackson

ISBN:1548164747
ISBN-13:97815487164744

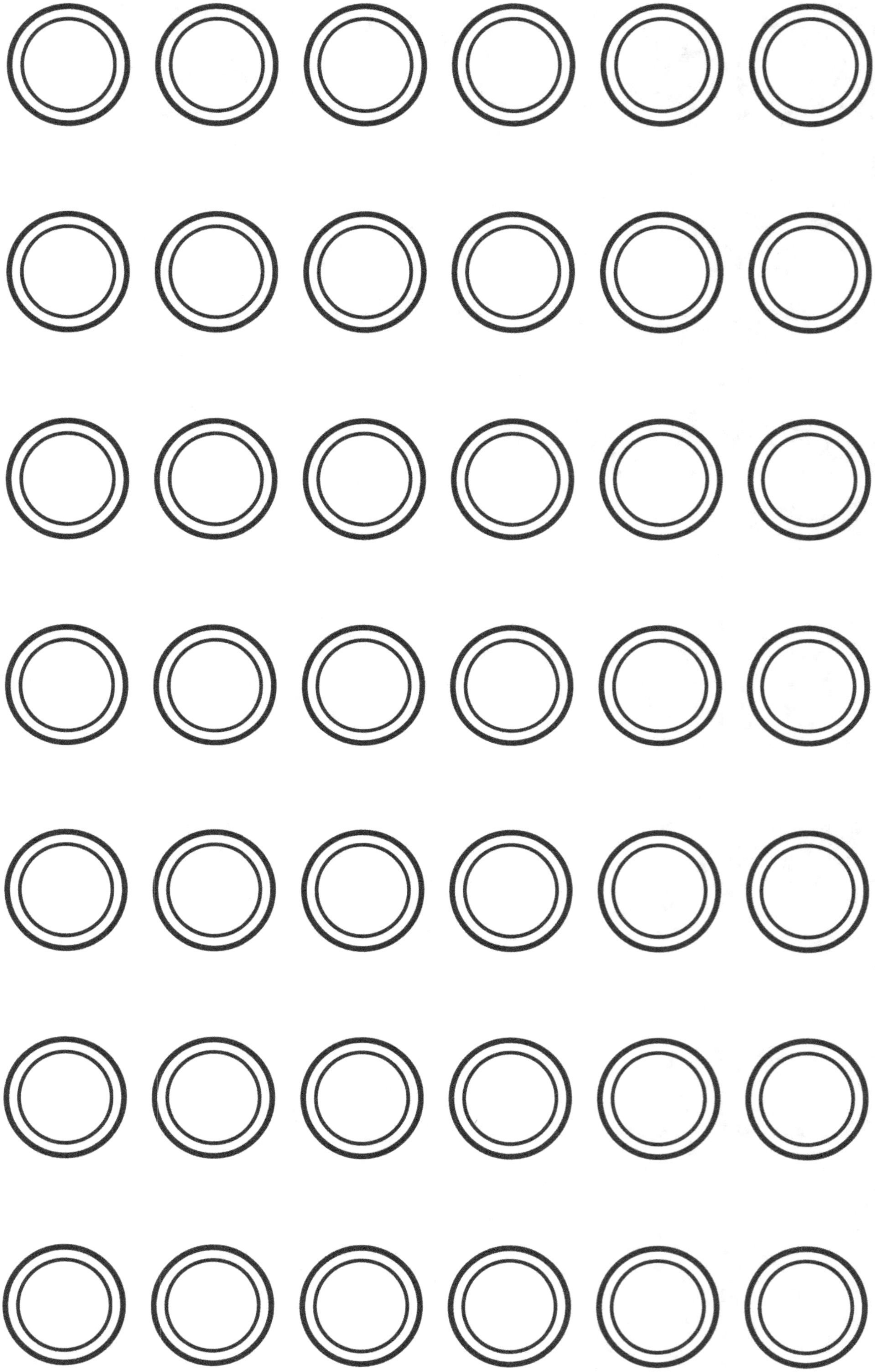

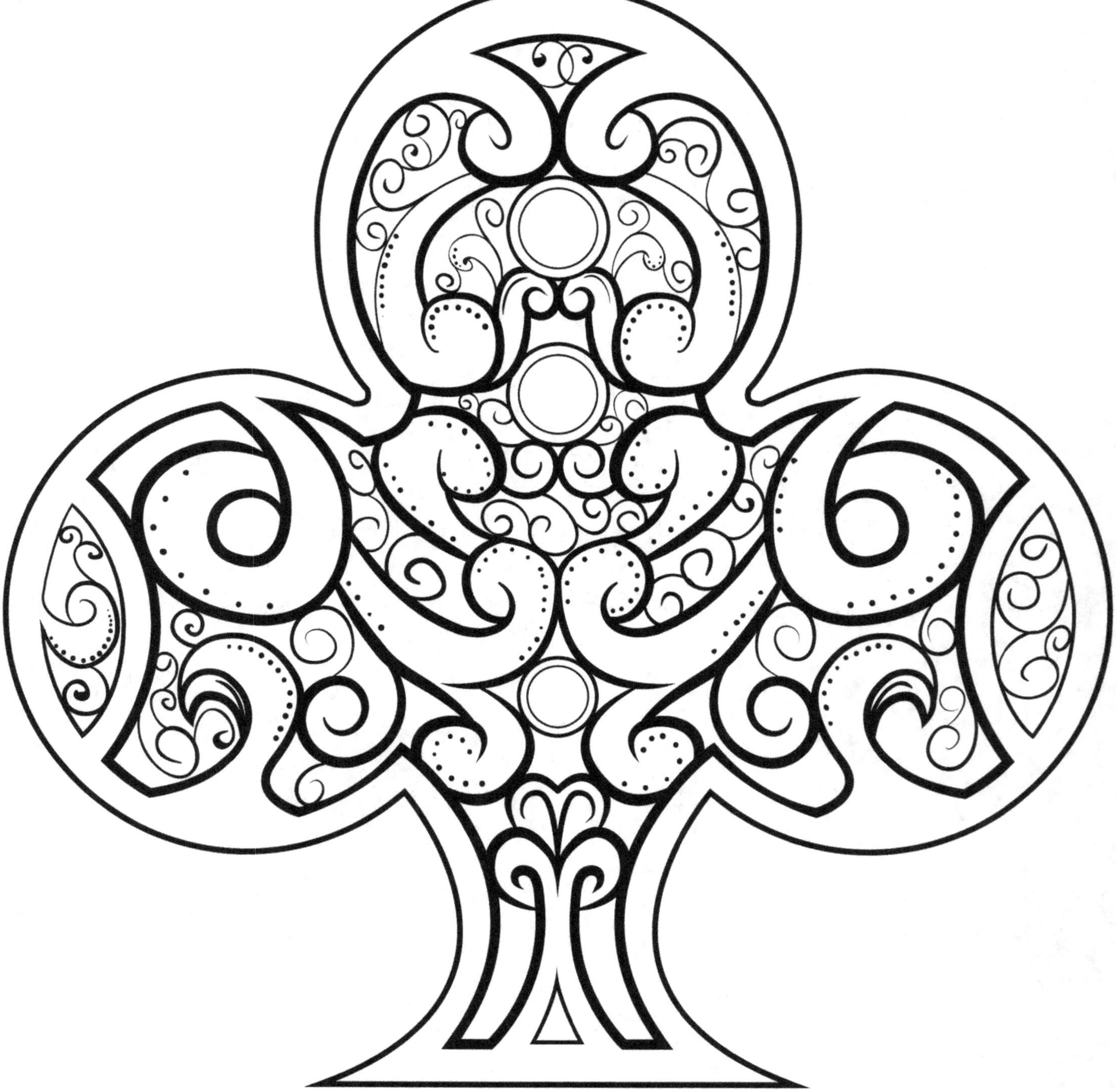

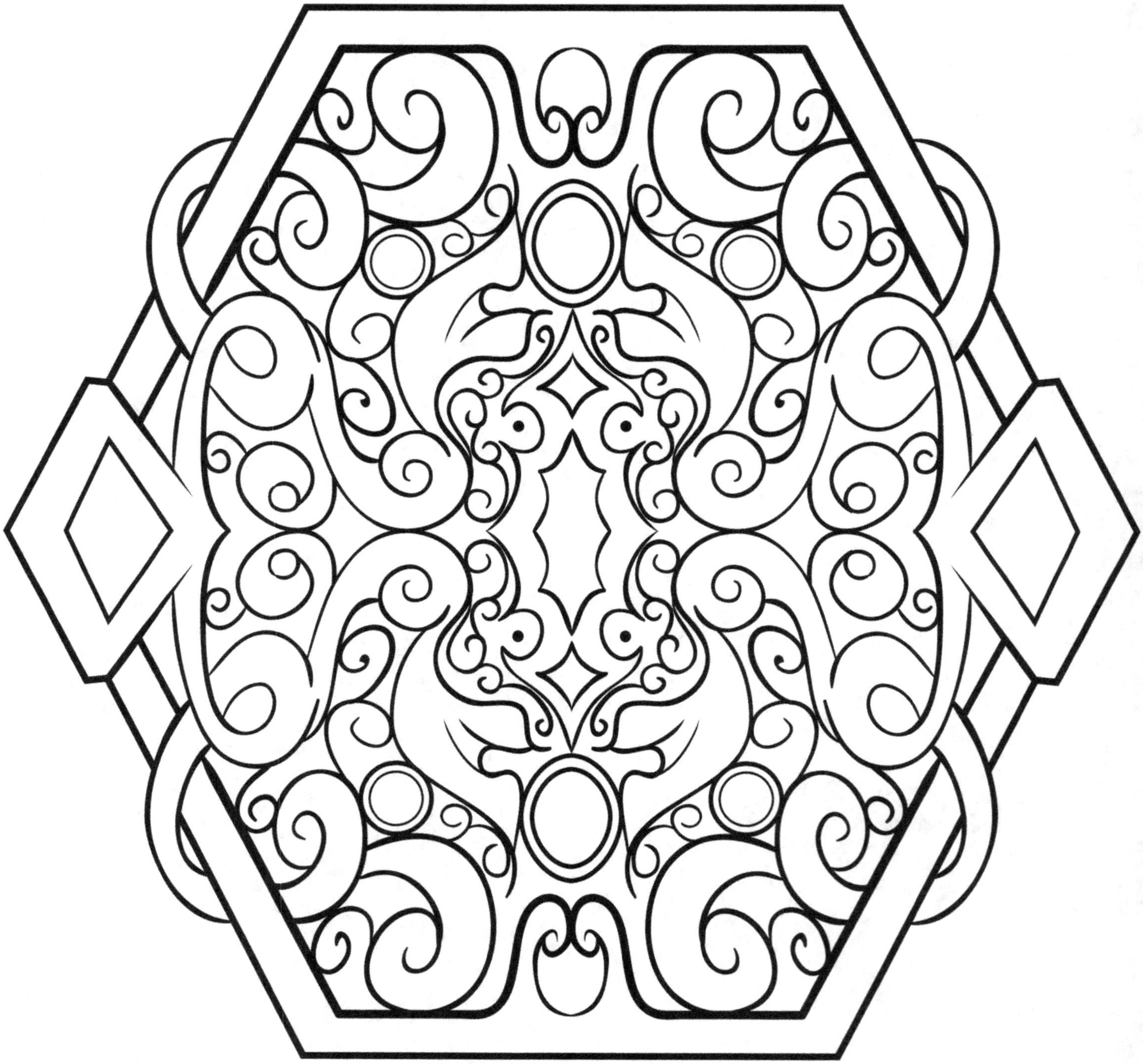

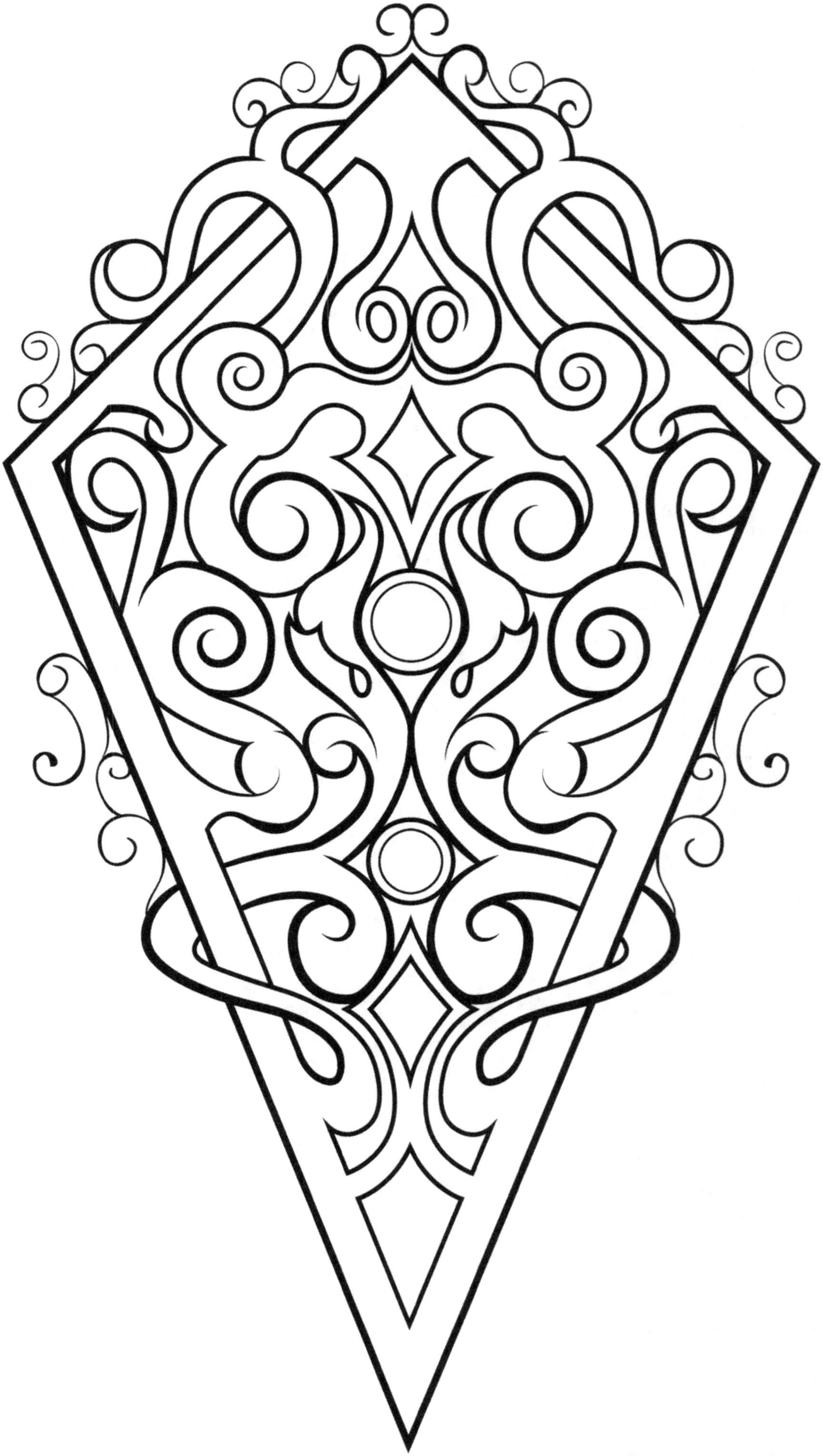

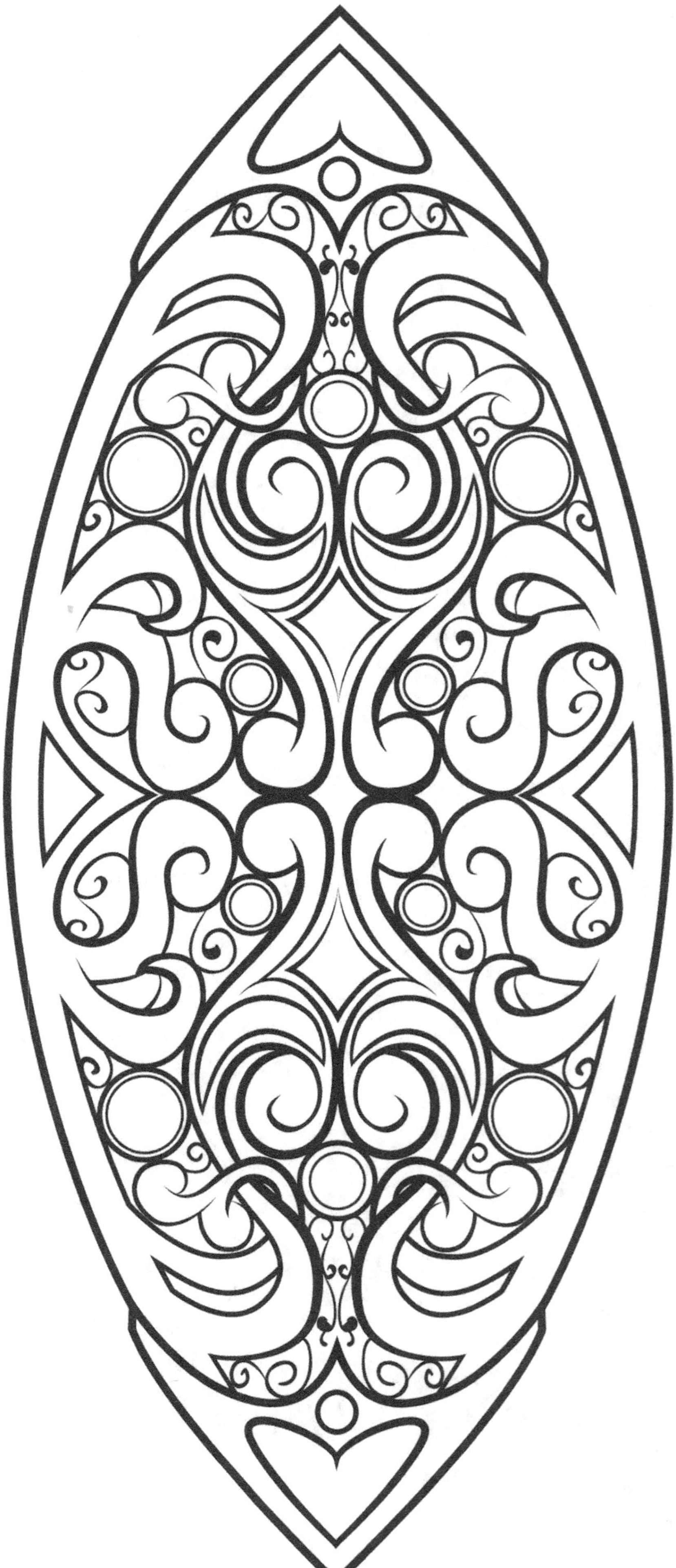

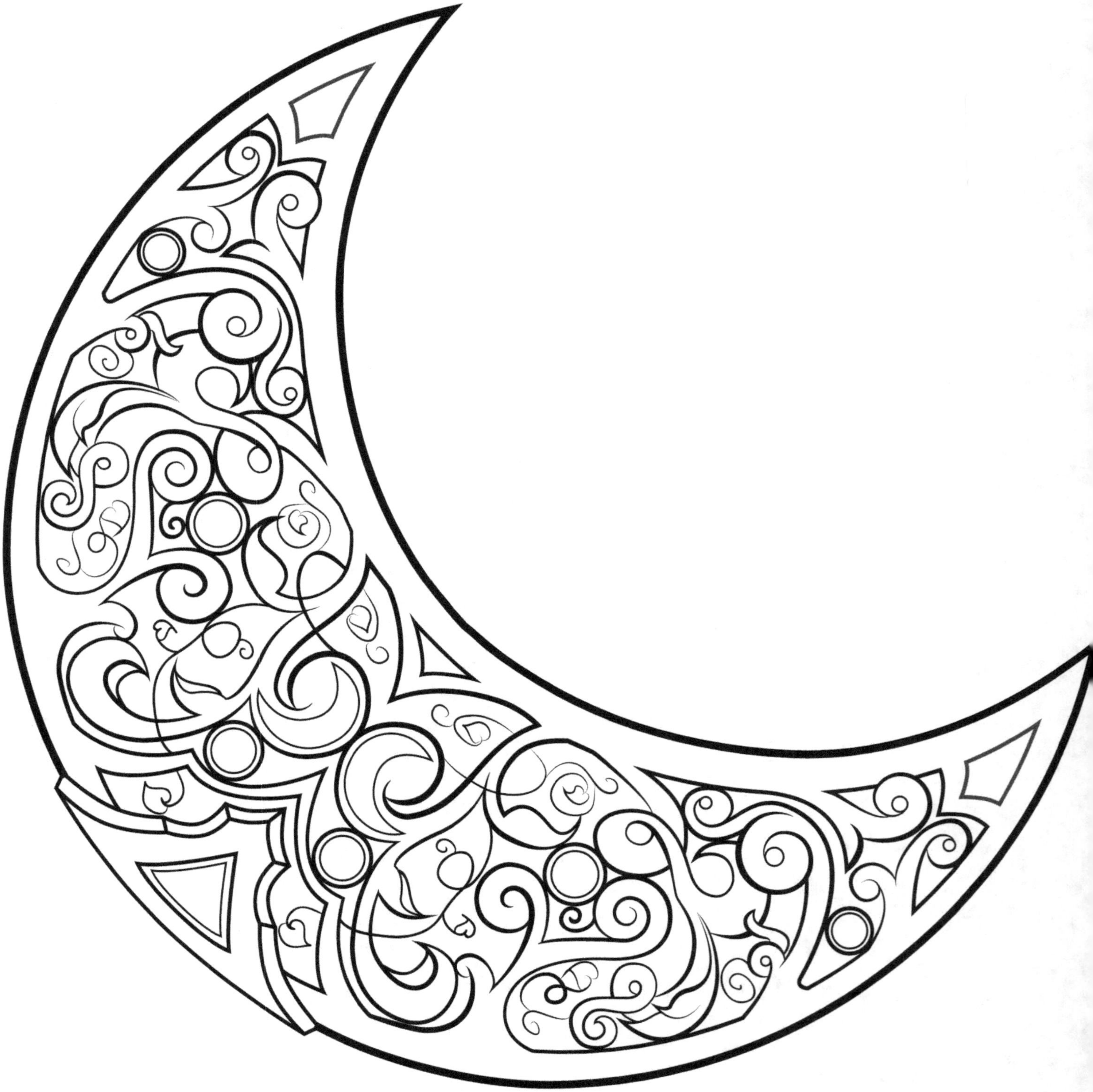

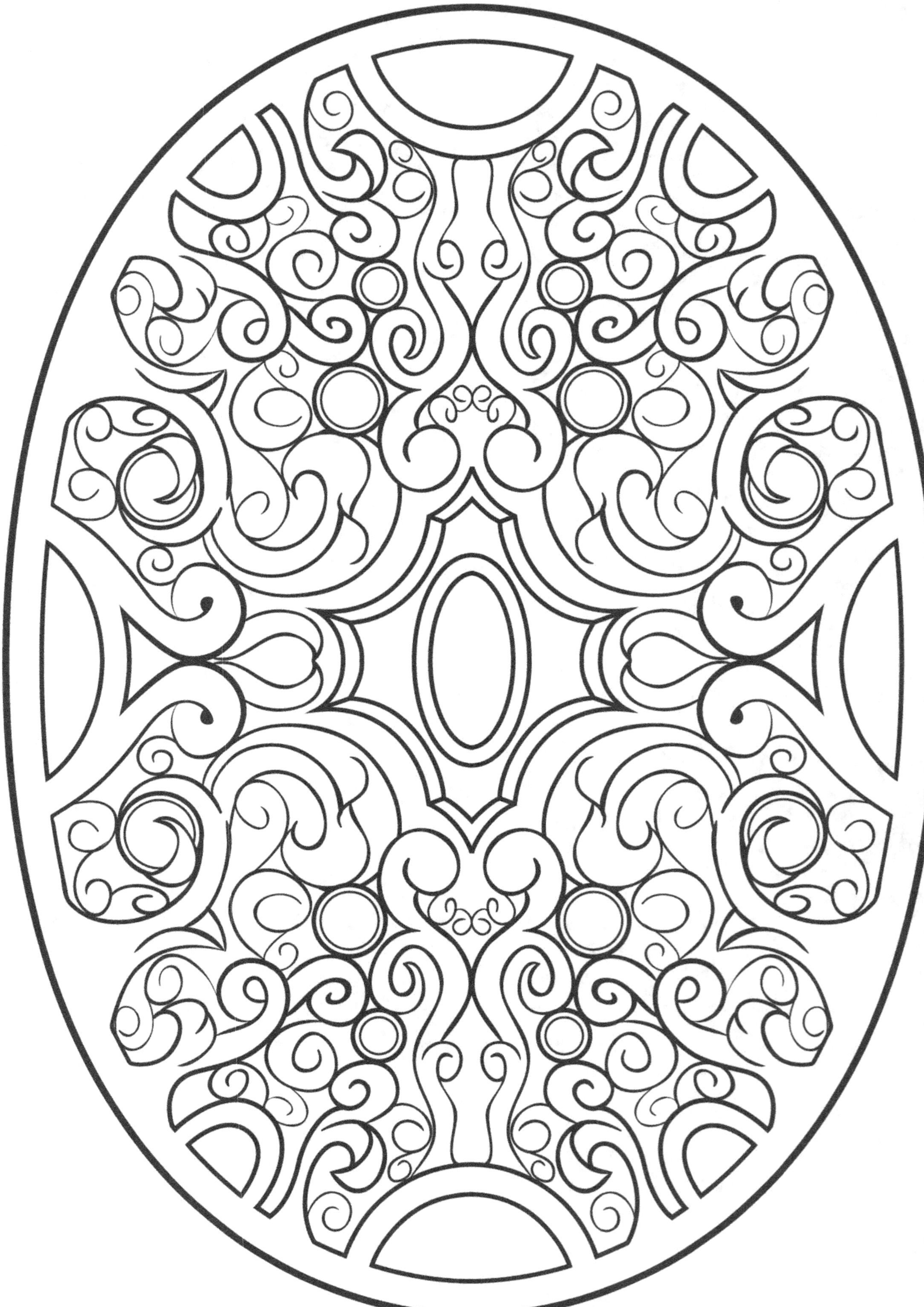

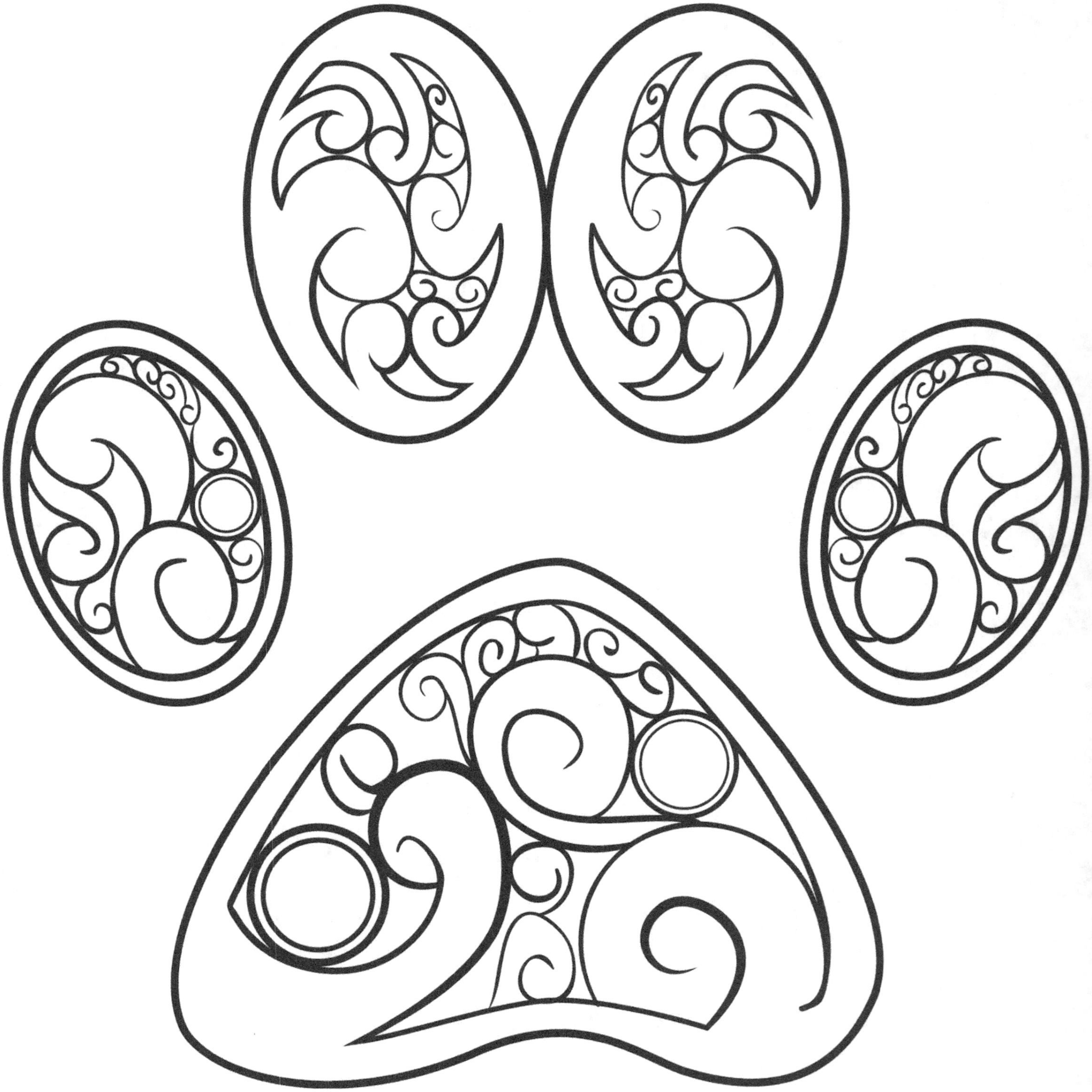

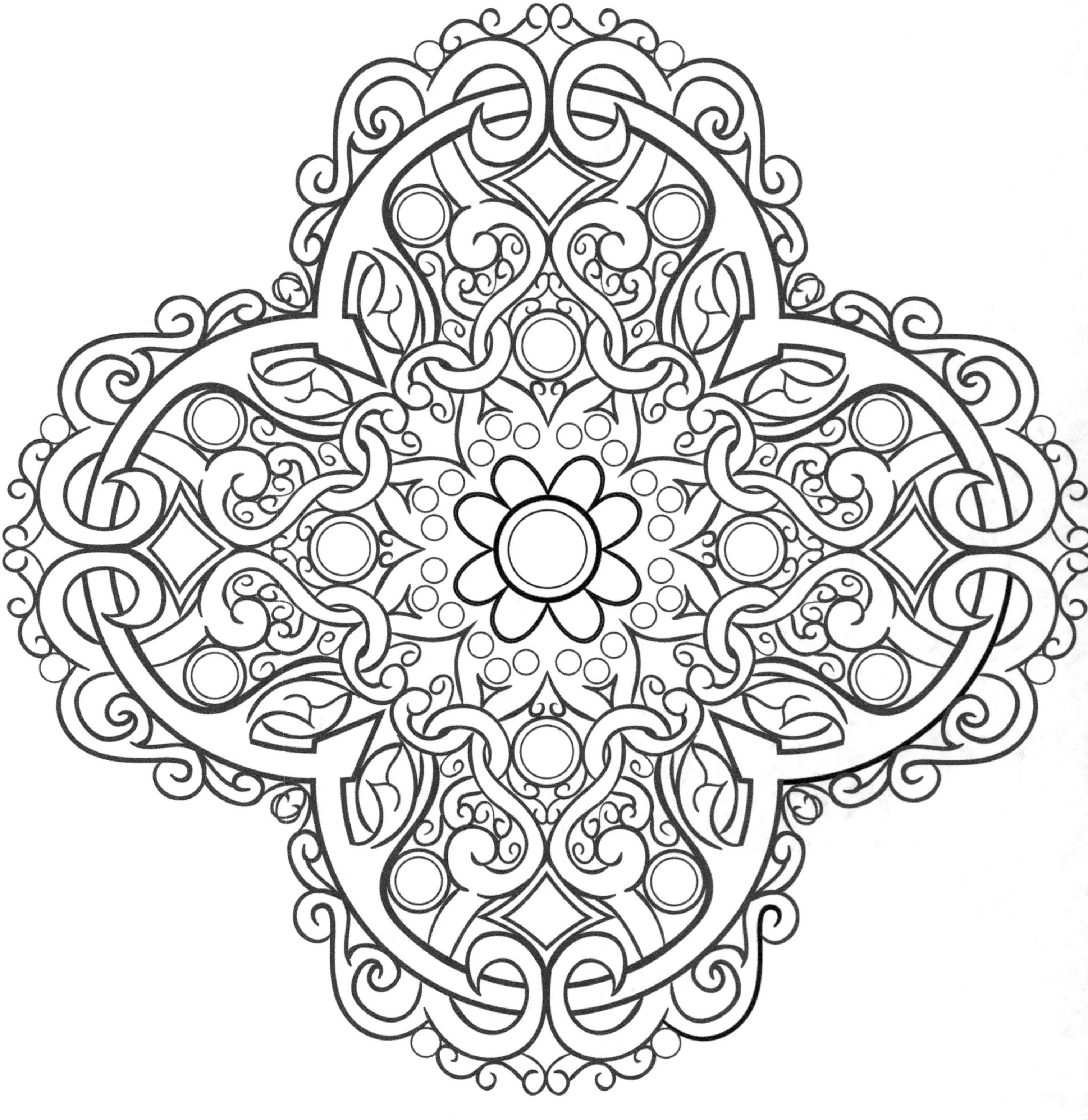

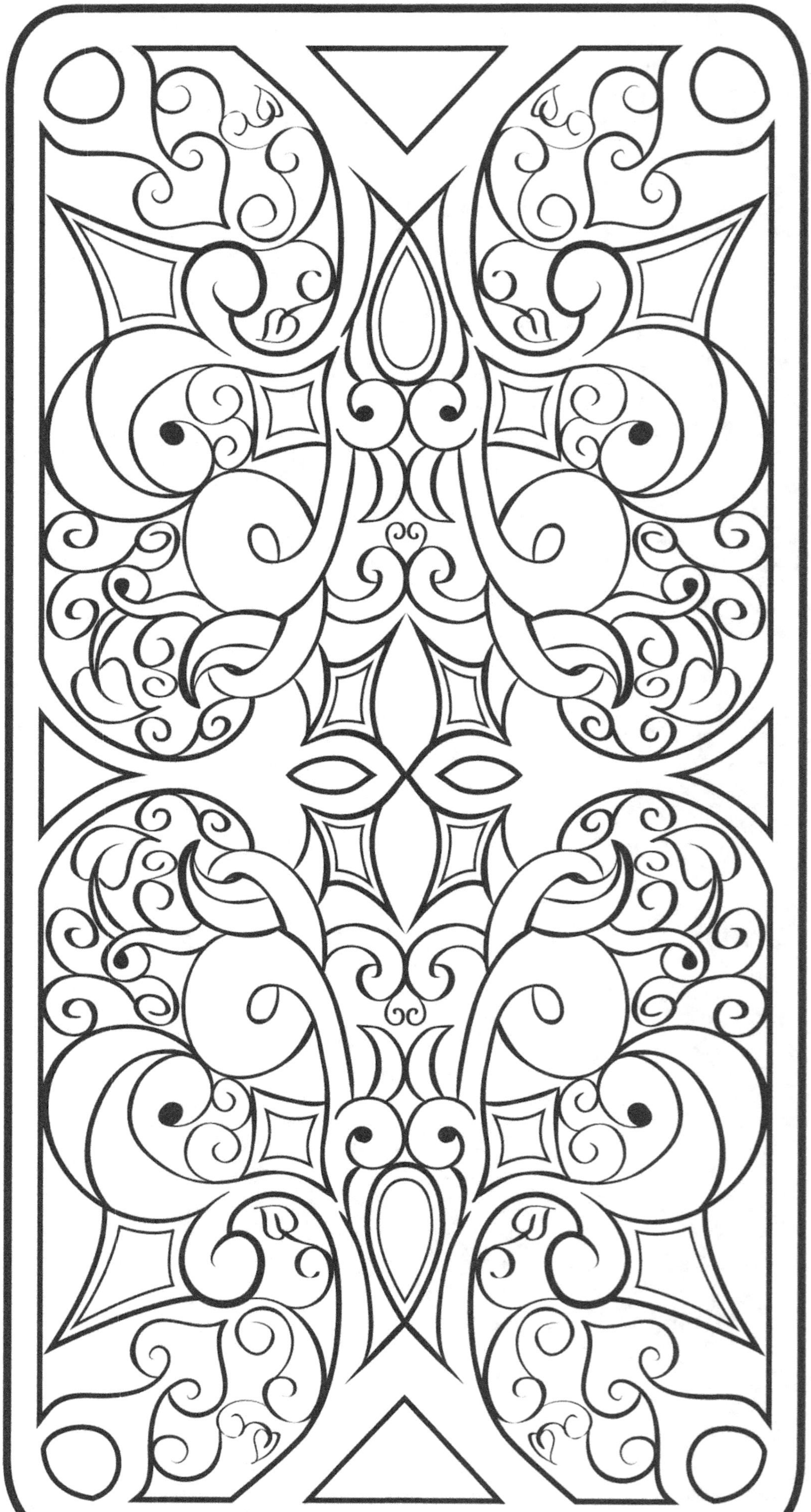

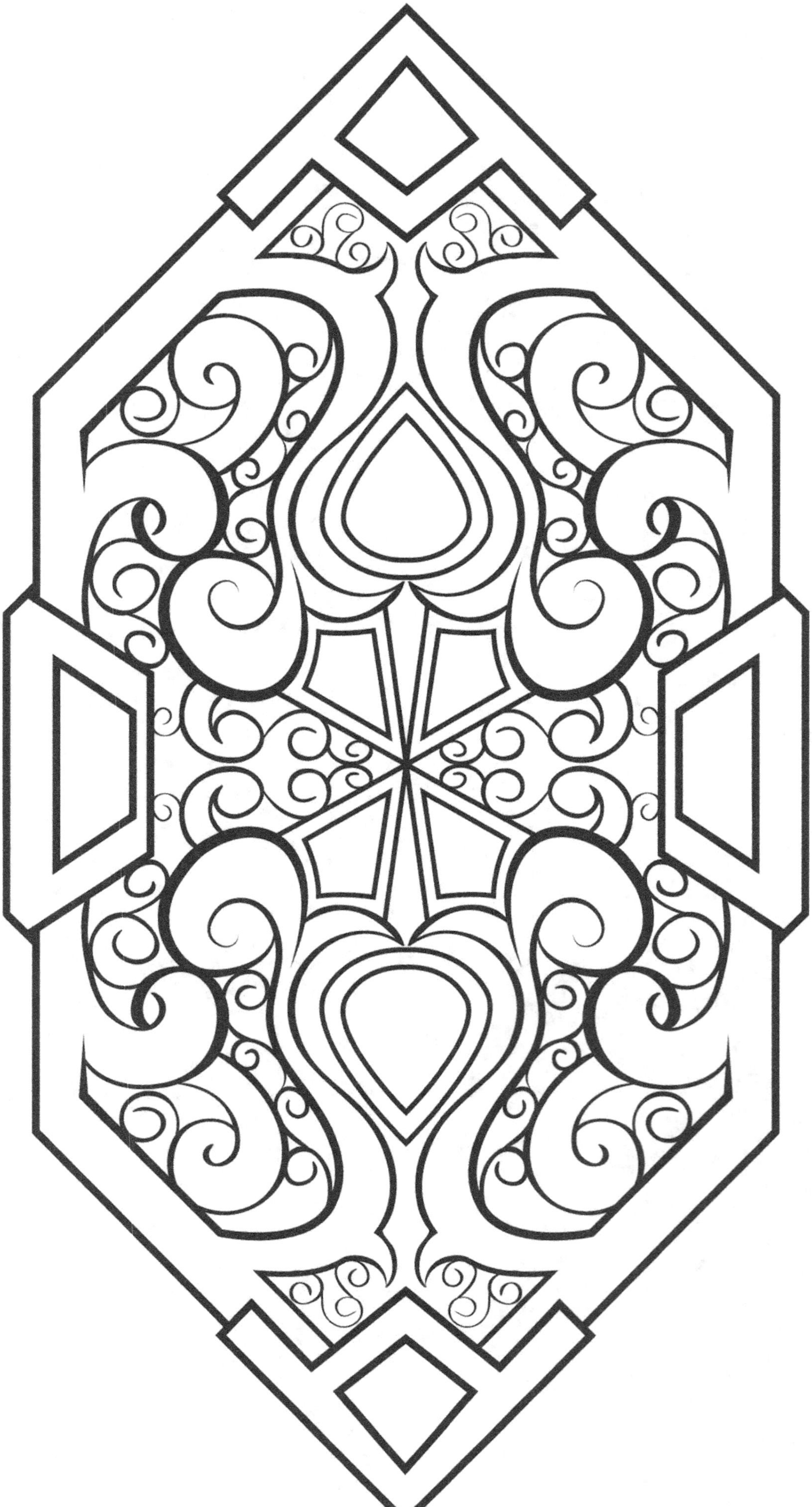

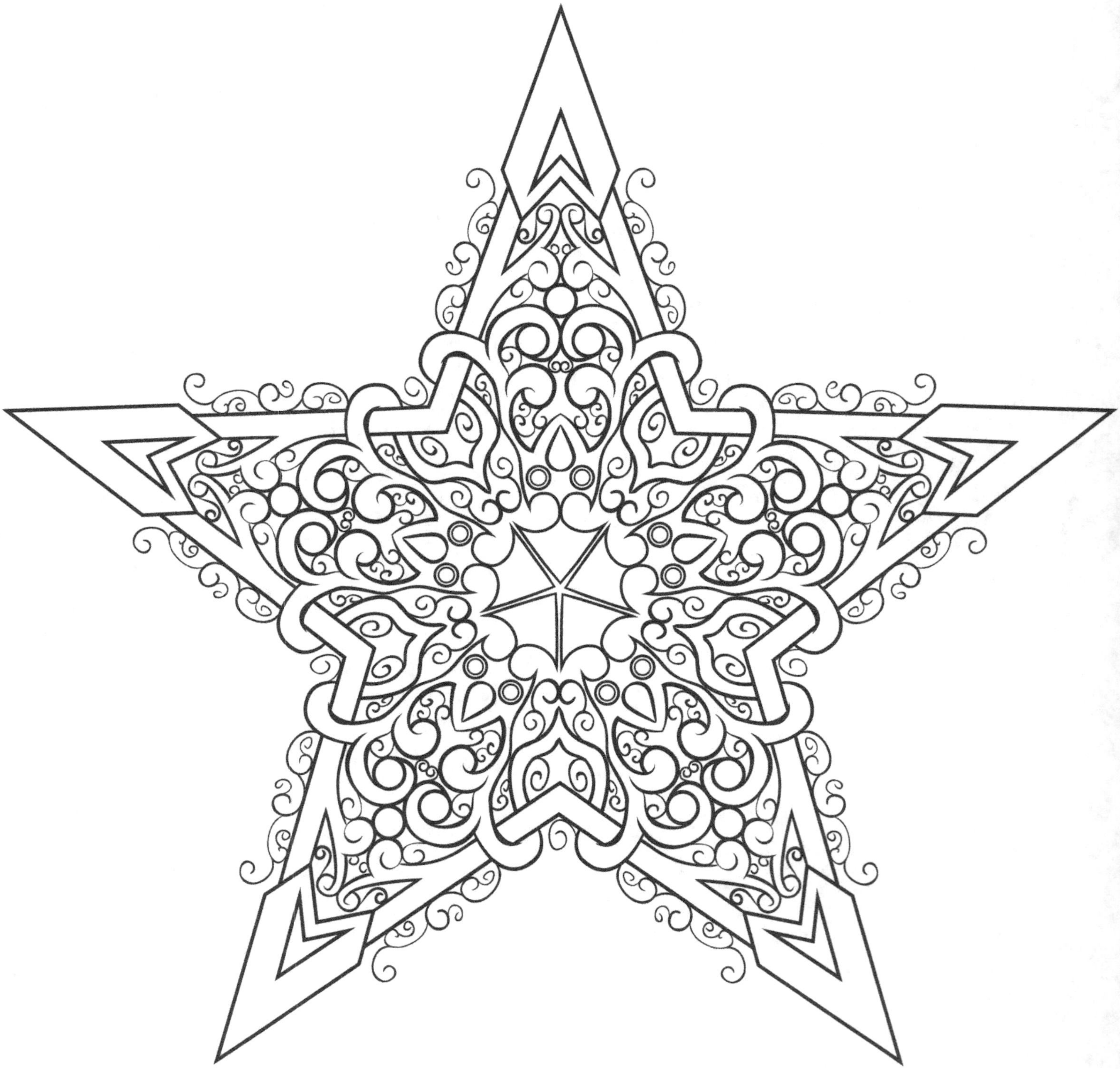

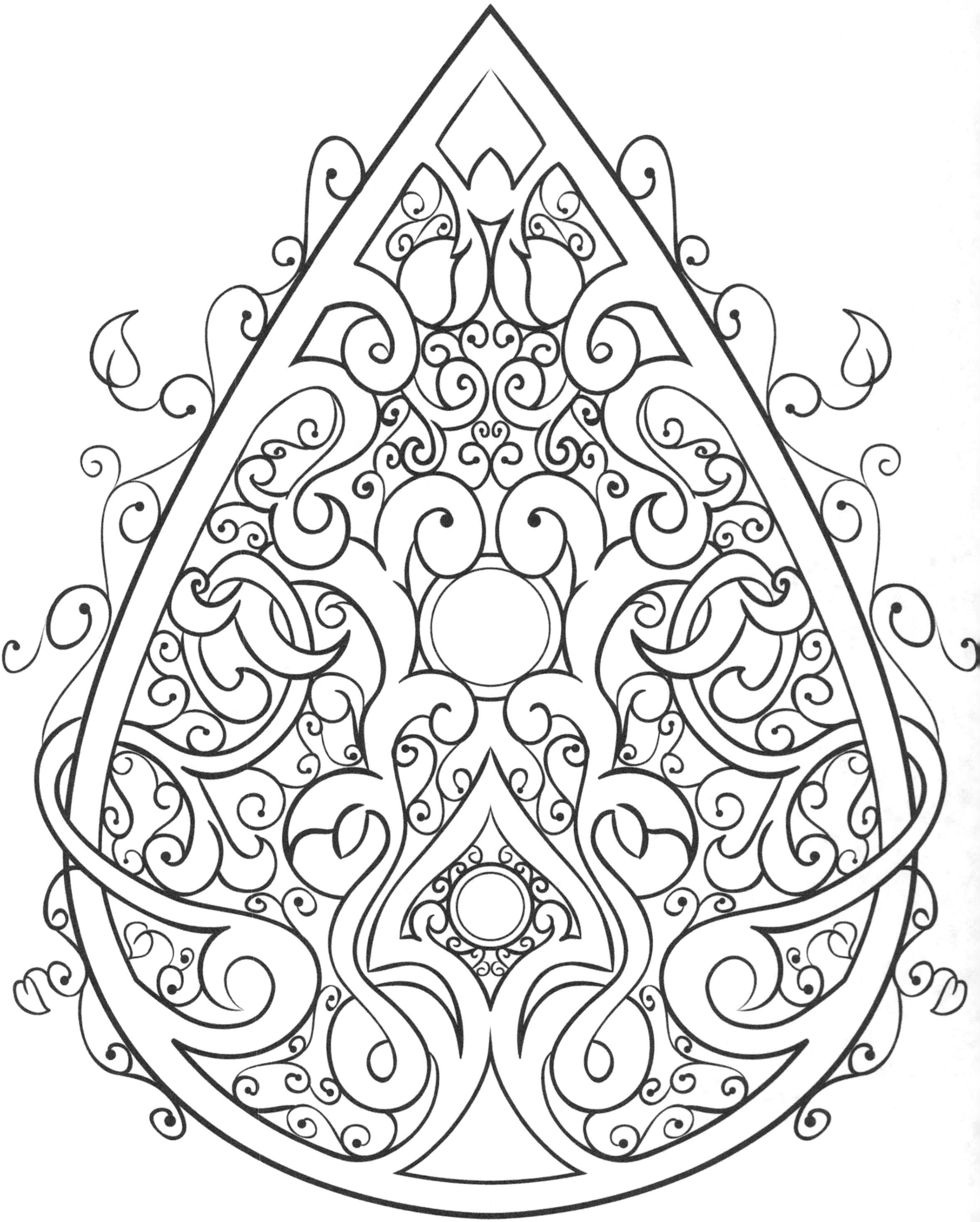

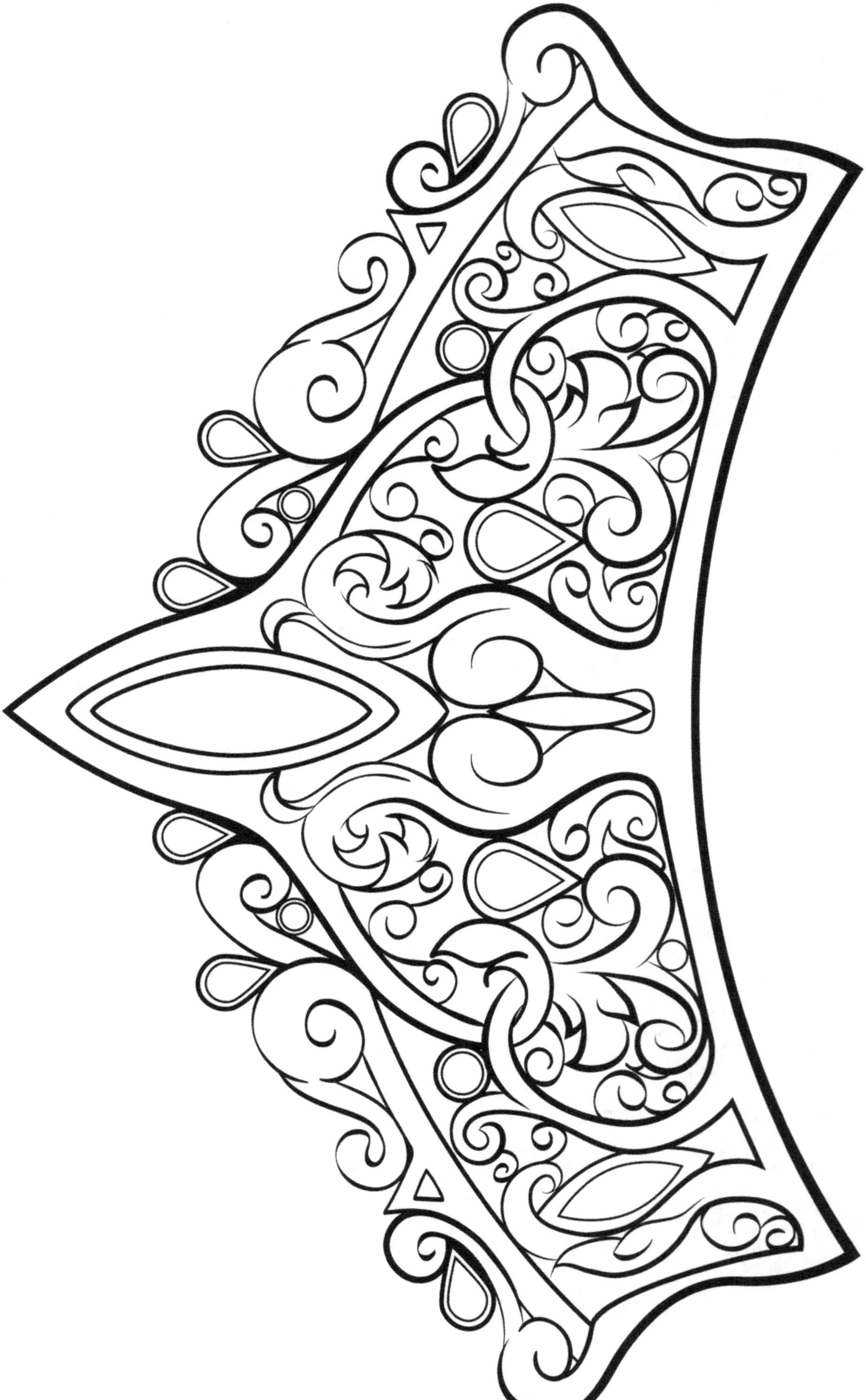

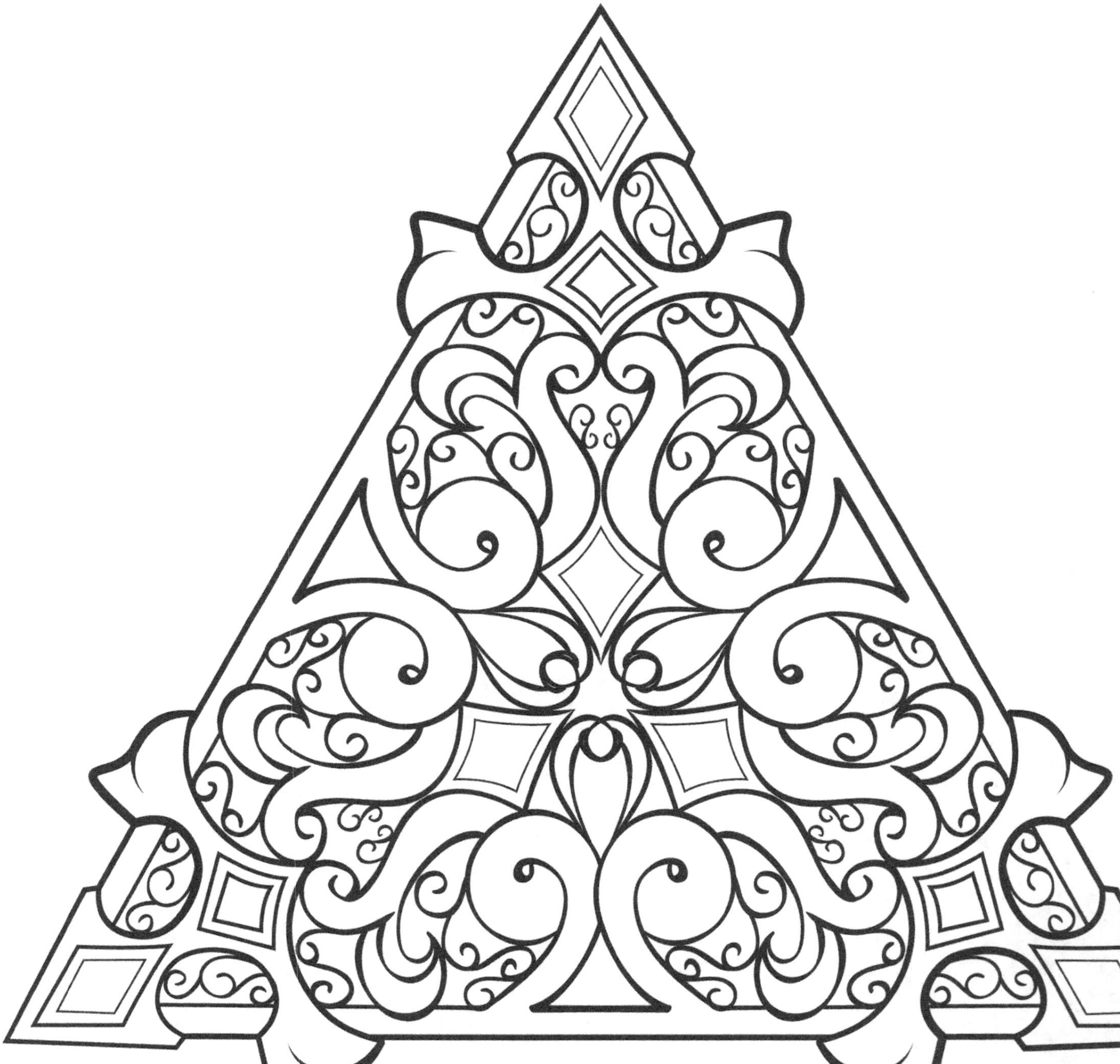

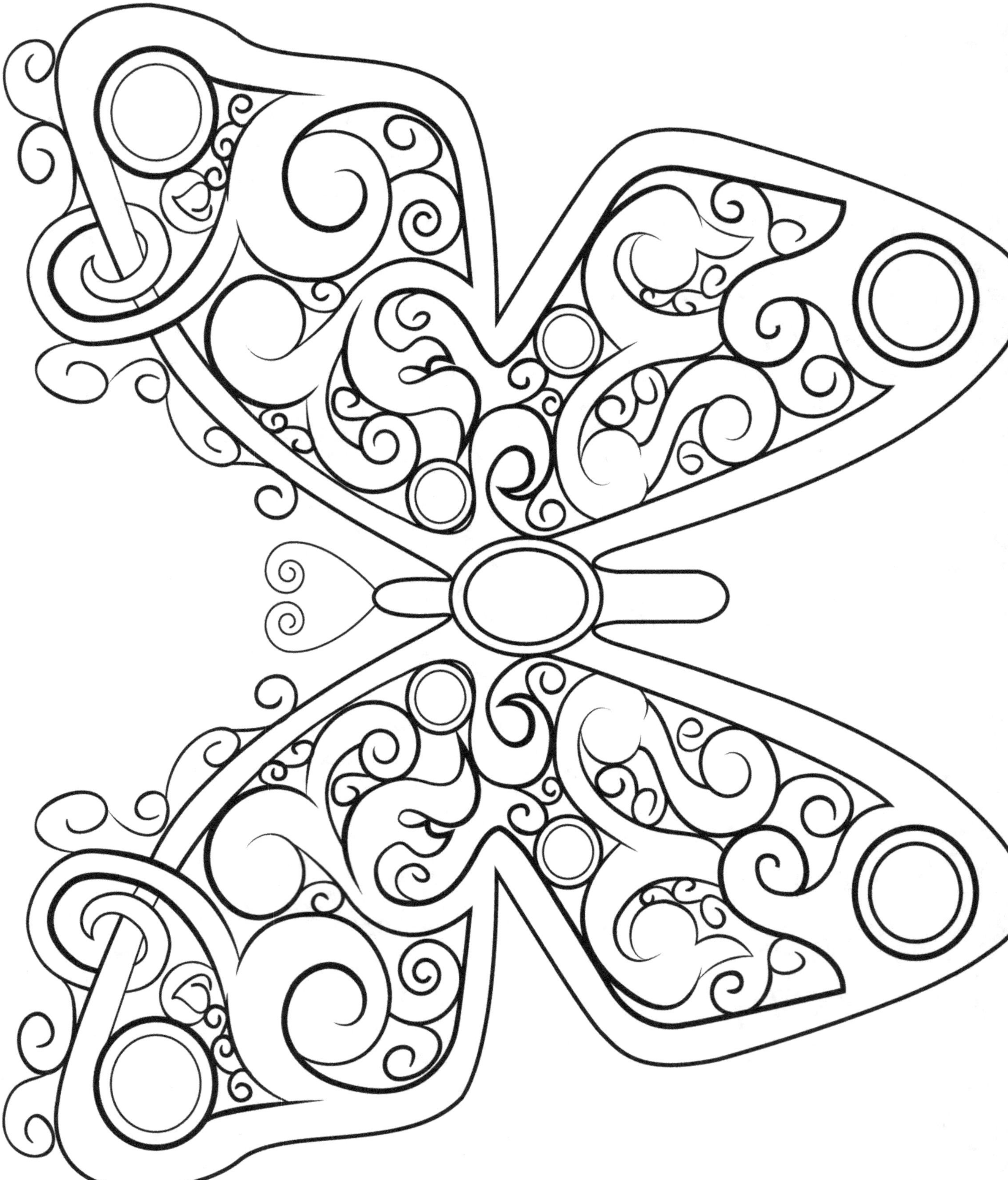

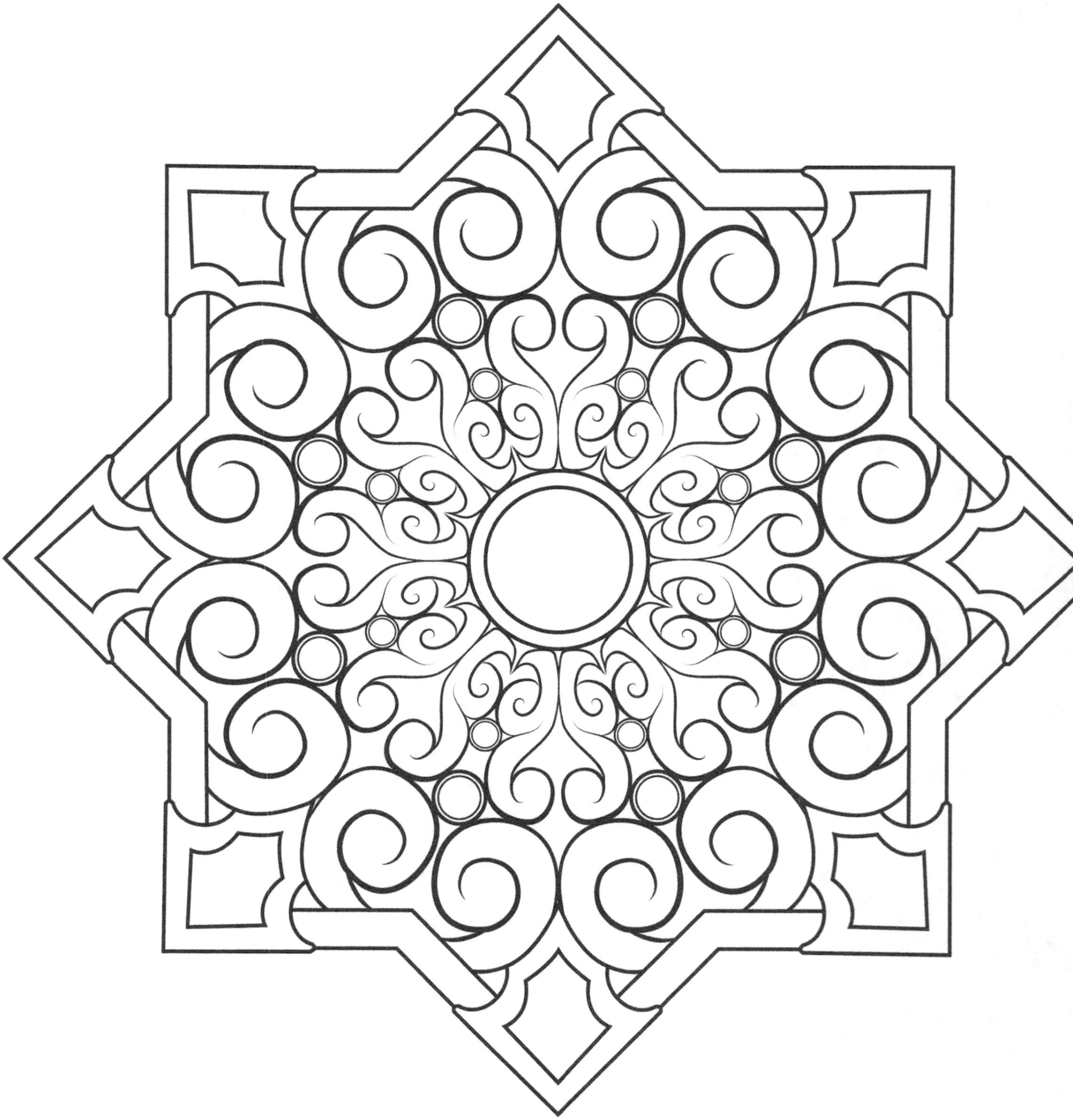

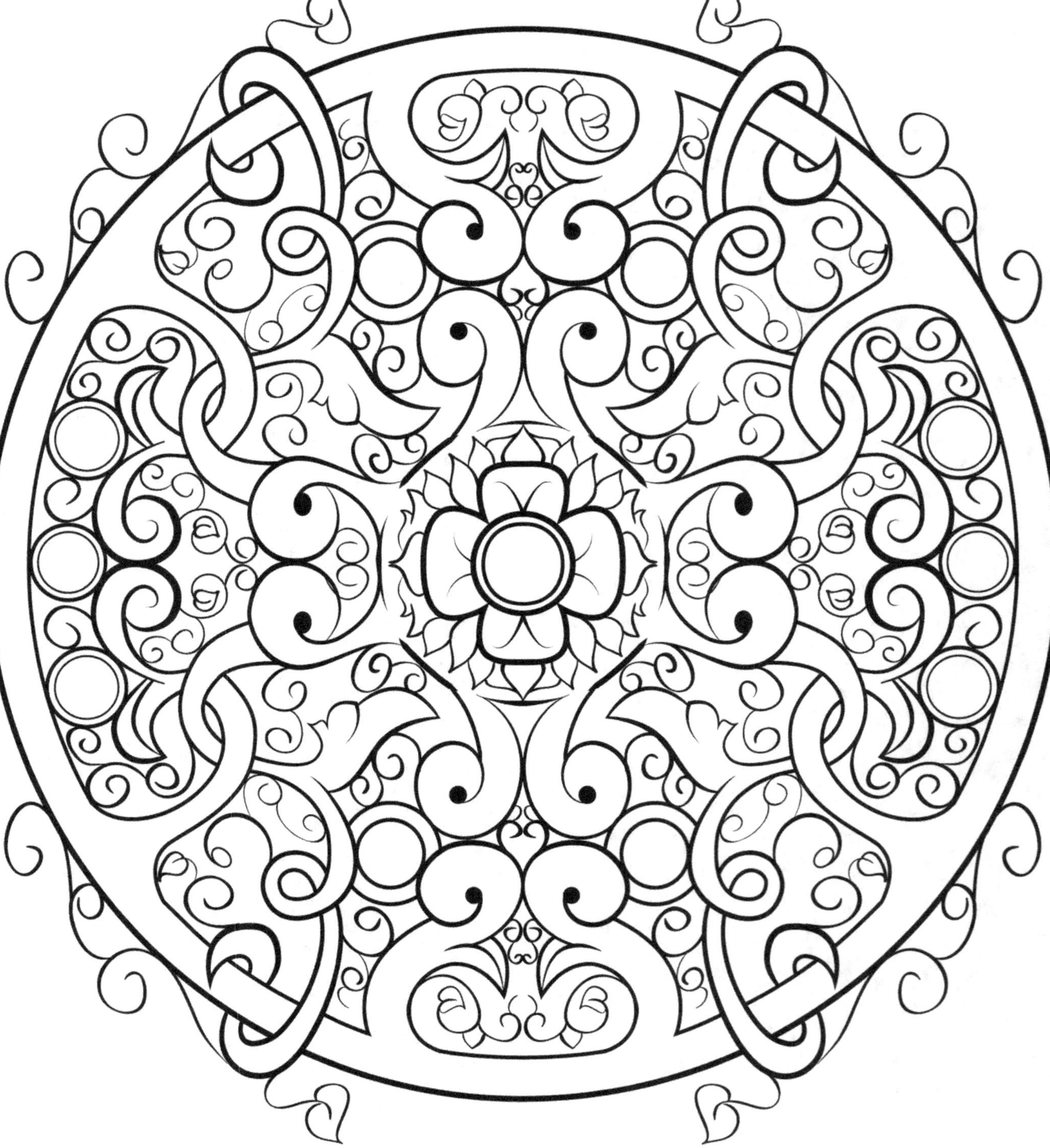

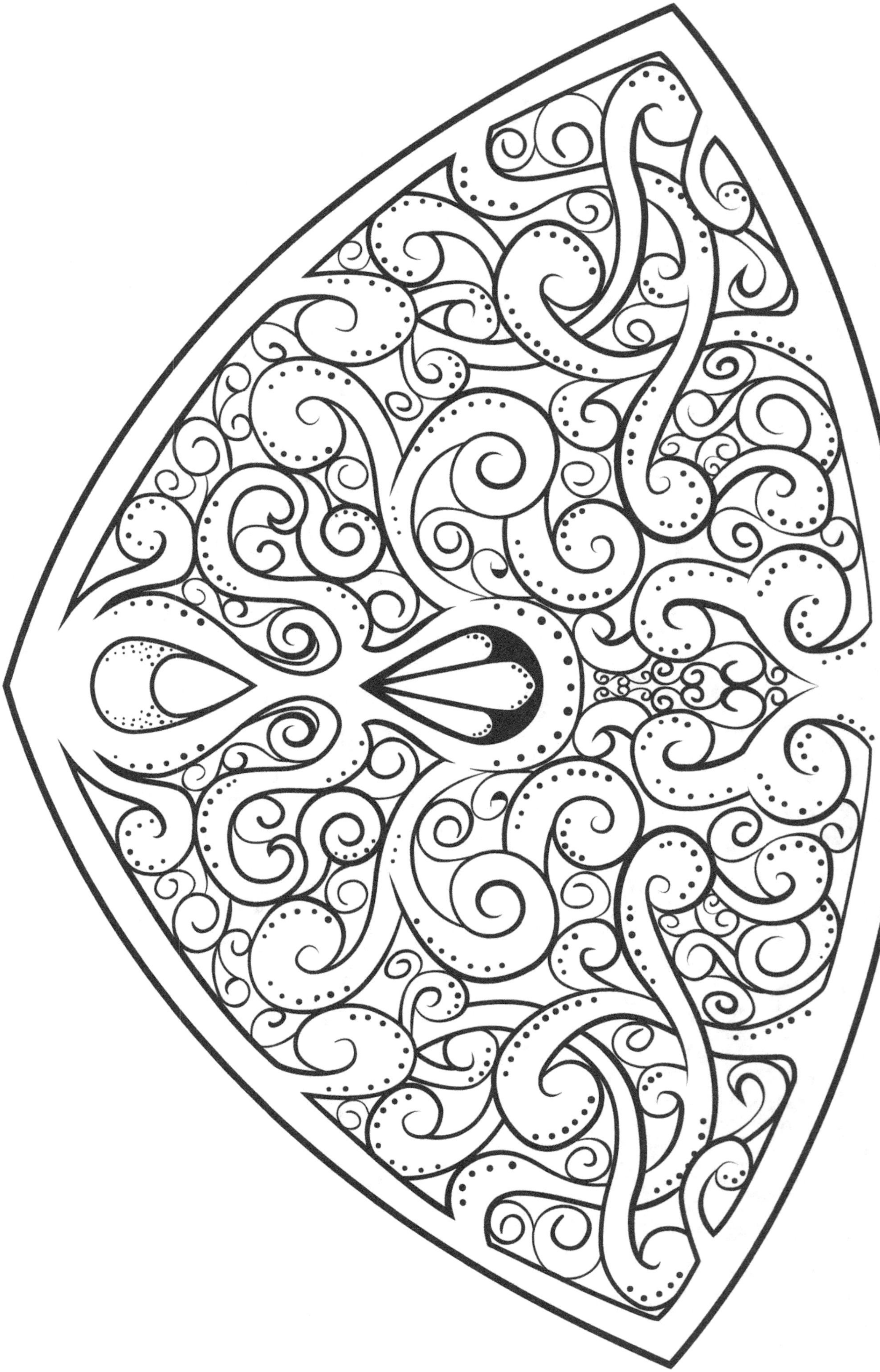

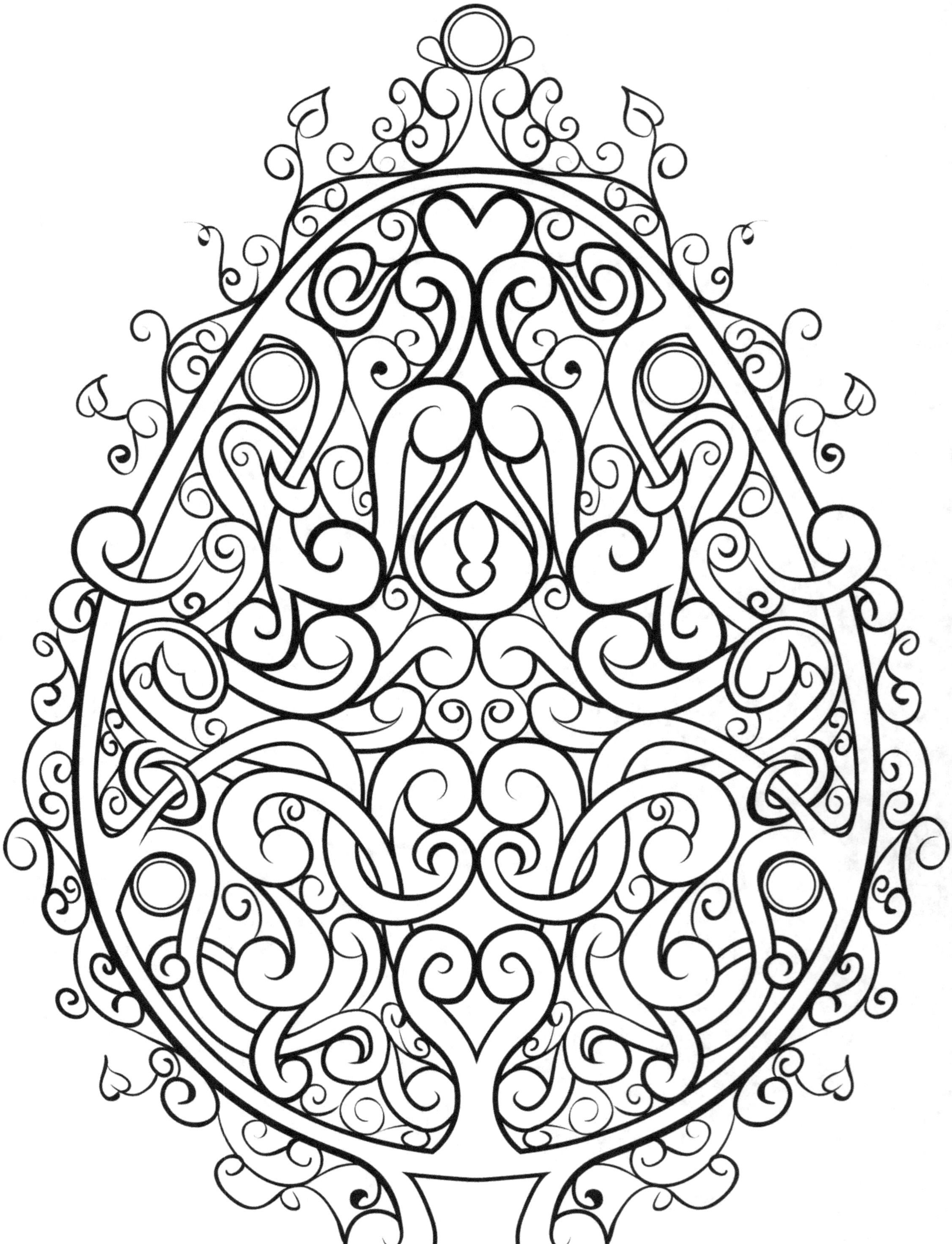

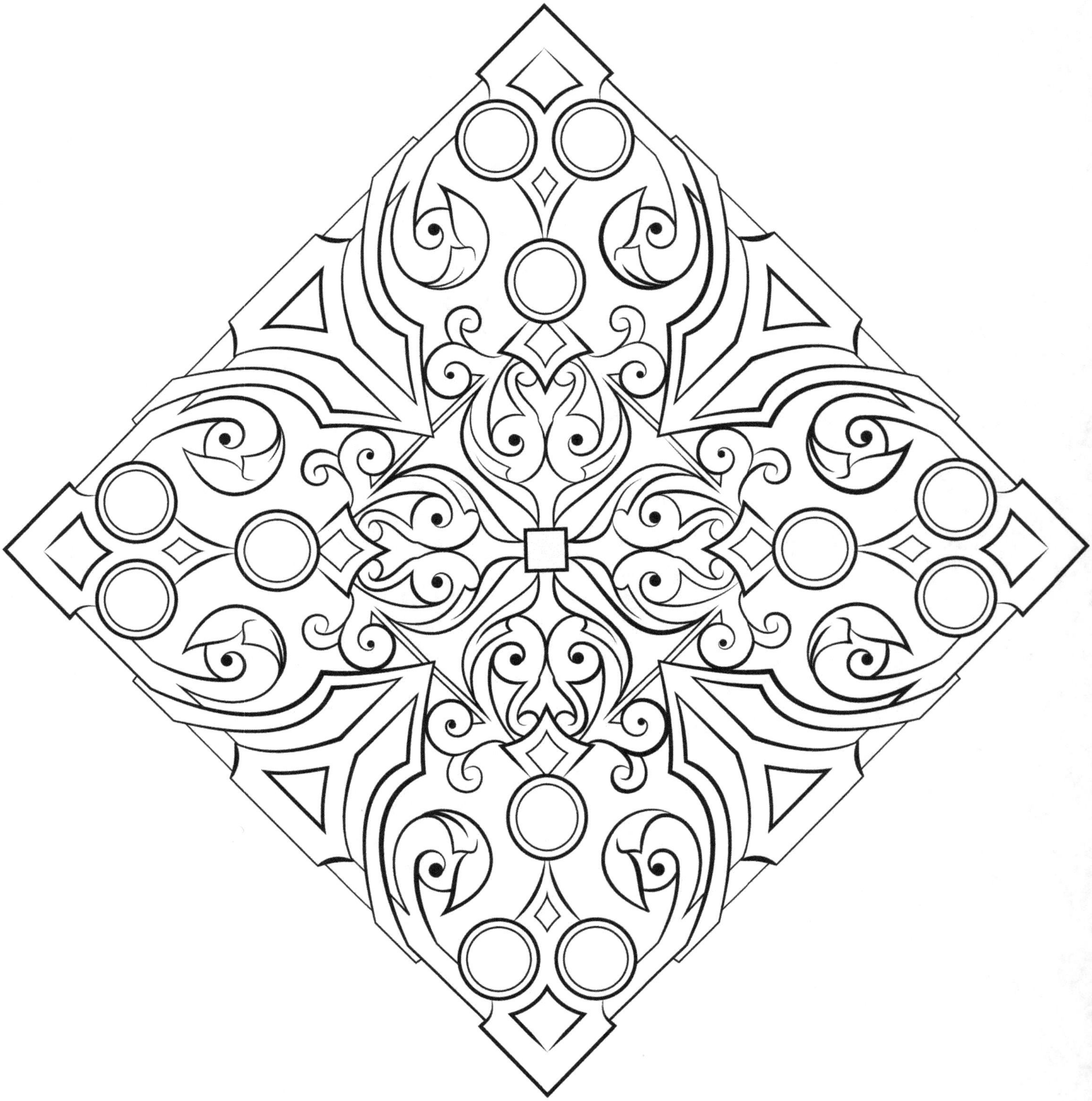

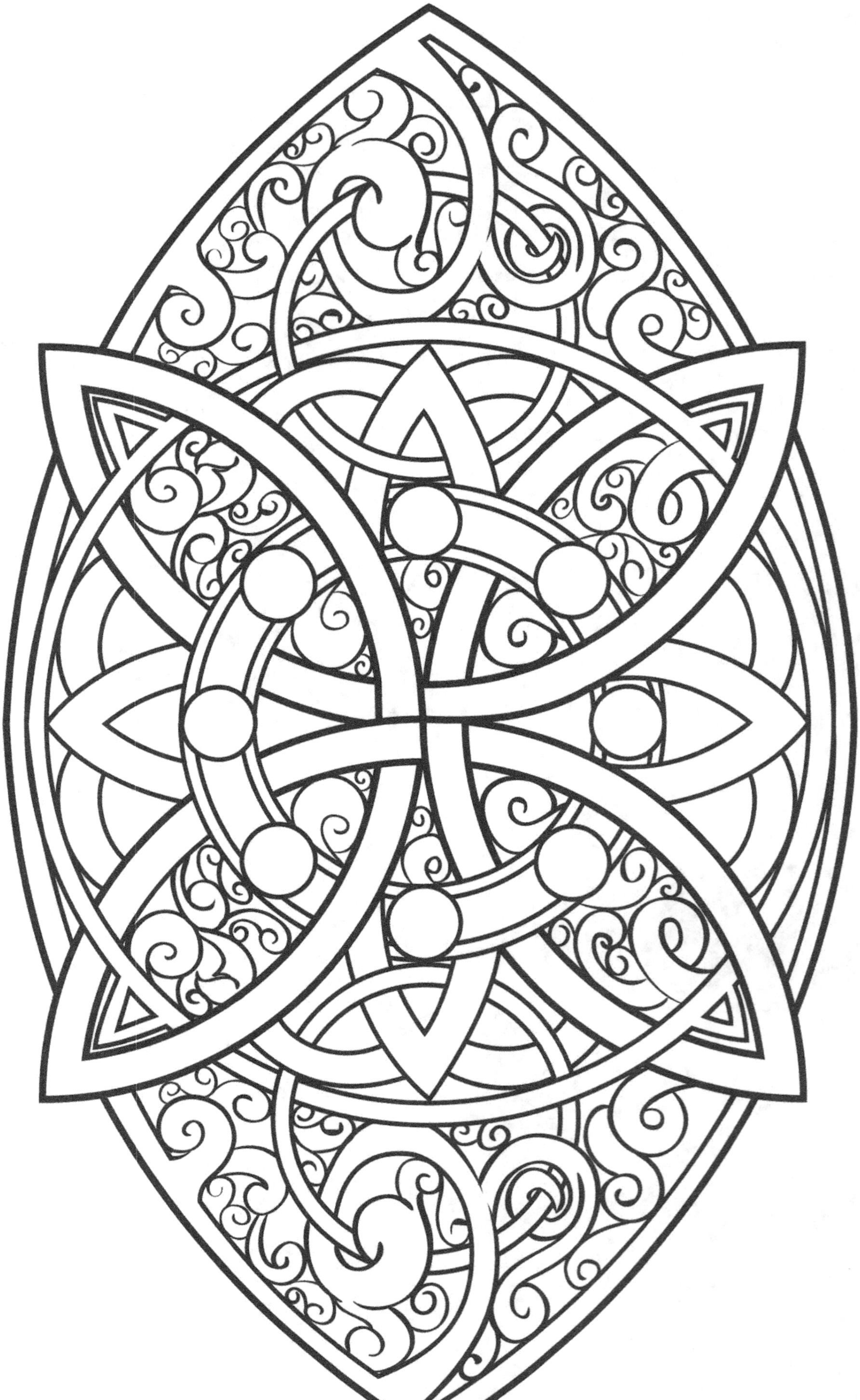

www.ingramcontent.com/pod-product-compliance
Lightning Source LLC
Chambersburg PA
CBHW081228170526
45165CB00009B/2992